T0117082

THE POTTER PRINCIPLES

THE SECRETS TO SUCCESSFUL BUSINESS RECRUITMENT

JENI FORMAN

IUNIVERSE, INC.
NEW YORK   BLOOMINGTON

The Potter Principles
The Secrets to Successful Business Recruitment

Copyright © 2009 by Jeni Forman

All rights reserved. No part of this book may be used or reproduced by any means, graphic, electronic, or mechanical, including photocopying, recording, taping or by any information storage retrieval system without the written permission of the publisher except in the case of brief quotations embodied in critical articles and reviews.

The views expressed in this work are solely those of the author and do not necessarily reflect the views of the publisher, and the publisher hereby disclaims any responsibility for them.

iUniverse books may be ordered through booksellers or by contacting:

iUniverse
1663 Liberty Drive
Bloomington, IN 47403
www.iuniverse.com
1-800-Authors (1-800-288-4677)

Because of the dynamic nature of the Internet, any Web addresses or links contained in this book may have changed since publication and may no longer be valid.

ISBN: 978-1-4401-7806-1 (sc)
ISBN: 978-1-4401-7808-5 (dj)
ISBN: 978-1-4401-7807-8 (ebk)

Printed in the United States of America

iUniverse rev. date: 12/9/2009

CONTENTS

PREFACE

The concept for the Potter Principles originated through a private, non-profit organization called the Inland Northwest Economic Alliance or INEA. Made up of eleven economic development groups from throughout Eastern Washington and Northern Idaho, INEA is a regional economic development initiative funded through a combination of public and private funding sources. Its Board of Directors is comprised of economic development professionals from throughout the region known as the Inland Northwest. The INEA and its supporters are continually looking for ways to educate and promote successful economic development initiatives to strengthen regional economies.

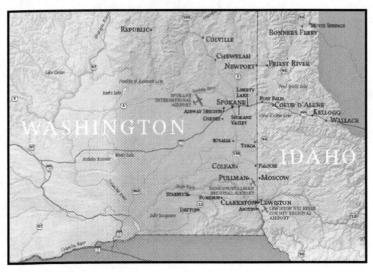

Initial efforts to form a regional organization to pursue business recruitment initiatives, such as the ones highlighted in this publication, were developed by Avista Corporation, a major private utility providing electric and natural gas services in many territories throughout the Inland Northwest. Historically, Avista (formerly Washington Water Power) has been a leader in helping to drive the economy of the Inland Northwest in new and innovative ways. Avista started this initiative by convening a group of private and public entities to consider the development of INEA. This group committed to funding the organization for a three-year period establishing the long-term commitment to the recruitment program. (A complete list of investors and partners can be found in the Acknowledgements at the end of this book.)

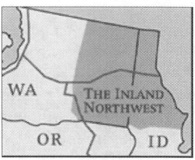

INEA membership geography

The primary function of INEA is to utilize marketing and recruitment efforts to improve the economic conditions of the Inland Northwest. Founded in 2004, INEA quickly gained a solid reputation in economic development circles by contracting with Bob Potter, a well-known, successful business recruiter, to handle its recruitment program. The organization's portfolio now contains nearly 100 companies, and INEA reported its first recruitment success in 2007.

INEA's financial and community partners are the primary supporters of this effort. INEA's members recognize the importance a successful business recruitment program plays as part of an overall economic development strategy. Through acknowledging these principles and reviewing these stories, the goal of this publication is to record Bob's recruitment methods so that others might glean ideas from his long-standing success. Whether a small community or a larger region is looking for job growth or economic diversification, business recruitment can be a key component leading to positive economic results, as Bob's legacy so aptly proves.

Read on to learn about Bob Potter's experiences and principles as a business recruiter. During his many years leading Jobs Plus -- the economic development organization representing the greater Coeur d'Alene area and Kootenai County in Northern Idaho -- and supporting INEA, Potter has enjoyed many recruitment successes.

PART I

THE MAN &
THE METHOD

1. Meet Bob Potter

Bob Potter, any relation to the famous Harry? No, not even a distant relative, but the methodology he uses to get businesses to relocate to the Inland Northwest is, nonetheless, magical. According to former Idaho Governor, Dirk Kempthorne, "Bob Potter made Potter famous long before Harry came along." Potter's success at creating economic diversity, in a region once overly-dependent upon mining and natural resources, has led some to complain he has been "too successful." Indeed, Bob Potter has had tremendous influence and a positive impact on virtually everything he has touched throughout his career.

Spanning a period of over 36 years, Bob enjoyed a very successful career with American Telephone Company and its divested entities. He served in various key positions both at the company's headquarters in New York City and New Jersey, as well as numerous field positions. In 1983, he became Sales Vice President for the Western Region of the United States and was responsible for the major markets.

Bob Potter © Journal Communications Inc.

Bob's career in telecommunications evolved through some of the industry's most tumultuous, not to mention historic, periods of transformation. Bob entered the field in 1951, after serving in the United States Marine Corps and attending Weber State College in Ogden, Utah, and the University of Utah in Salt Lake City. He was quickly identified as a leader who could successfully function in an environment of not only constant change, but also dramatic change.

Bob was often selected to manage new and different projects. His list of accomplishments within the company is impressive, and his strong leadership role in developing and implementing sales plans and strategies for AT&T Communications helped make this newly formed unit of the corporation a tremendous success.

When AT&T redefined its objectives and moved toward establishing a focus on marketing in addition to manufacturing, Bob played a key role in developing and implementing the strategy of bringing AT&T into the competitive market. He helped introduce the functions of market management, as well as sales management, into the newly expanded corporation's hierarchy.

Bob was given the responsibility of forming and managing the large markets in the Western Region. This task involved bringing together those entities that would be needed for market penetration into the Mountain States, Pacific Coastal and Northwest States, including Alaska and Hawaii. The task also involved managing the complex divestiture process with Pacific Telephone, Pacific Northwest Bell and Mountain Bell.

After retiring from AT&T, Bob accepted the position of President and Chief Operating Officer of Incomnet, Inc., based in Los Angeles. Incomnet manufactured message servicing computers in the United States and India and operated two networks in the United States. According to Bob, one of the best highlights of this job involved several trips to India in order to upgrade the India Telegraph system. Potter led Incomnet for almost two years. "I should have done more due diligence before I started with Incomnet. It was very interesting and the company had lots of potential, but we were ten years ahead of our time," says Bob. "It was a great learning experience, but my main goal when I started was to get someone positioned to serve as the president. Once that was accomplished, I was ready to leave and look for a place to retire."

How did Bob end up in North Idaho? He discovered the area while visiting his daughter at Whitworth University in Spokane, Washington, during the mid 1980s. Bob and his wife, Pat, of 55 years, wanted a house on the water. They looked at a lot of places, mostly on the East and West Coasts. "While our daughter was attending Whitworth College, I flew out to meet her one weekend," remembers Bob. "She and I got in the car to go for a drive over to Idaho. We drove around Coeur d'Alene Lake and I knew this was where Pat and I should buy a house and live."

After this trip, Bob went back to New Jersey and talked to Pat about what he and his daughter had found in North Idaho. "She said anywhere was fine with her as long as it wasn't more than one hour away from a Nordstrom," recalls Bob. "Amazingly enough I found out there was a Nordstrom in downtown Spokane, just 40 miles away. So the next time I was out visiting my daughter, I wandered over to Idaho again and ended up at Hayden Lake."

Bob didn't know it, but during this same time various private companies and individuals were organizing a new economic development initiative that would become Jobs Plus. Just three months after moving to Hayden Lake, their paths crossed. Starting from scratch at Jobs Plus in 1987, with little more than basic instinct for the job and five years worth of funding, Potter quickly found success in this new arena.

Today, some people think of Bob Potter as one of the 21st century's most successful big game hunters with his quarry being successful, well-paying, privately-owned corporations that are willing to relocate. His past work is, in part, responsible for the fact that Coeur d'Alene is now ranked #4 in Inc. Magazine's, May, 2008 list of Hottest Small Cities (those with an employment base of less than 150,000).

During Bob's 15 year career at Jobs Plus, he was responsible for recruiting more than 70 companies (of which 66 are family-owned and most of which were from California). These companies have contributed significantly to the local and regional economies by bringing the region:

> - Over $325 million in capital investment;
> - Nearly $100 million in annual payroll;
> - In excess of 3,900 jobs; and
> - More than $2.4 million in property taxes.

Potter calls his recruits "*an economic development annuity program*". "Basically, I'm a lazy salesman. I want to go where I have the best chance for success, that's why I focus primarily on California," says Bob. "More importantly, I didn't want to just create a job for myself; I wanted to be proud of something I did. And I wanted to help bring jobs here so we can get our kids to stay here, or at least be able to come back here to raise their families." The first company Potter recruited to relocate to North Idaho was US Products, a manufacturer of rug cleaning equipment from Canoga Park, CA. They relocated in 1989, and today US Products is recognized as a very successful company in the region.

On February 28, 2002, Bob Potter was recognized in Washington D.C. by the US Congress for his distinguished accomplishments at Jobs Plus. The congressional record on this day as entered by Idaho State Representative Butch Otter reads as follows:

> *" ...I rise today to bring to the attention of the House the distinguished accomplishments of Mr. Bob Potter of Hayden Lake, Idaho. Bob has been the President of Jobs Plus in Coeur d'Alene since the organization's inception 15 years ago. Known affectionately as "Mr. Jobs Plus," Bob's mission is to create investment and bring new jobs and companies to the Coeur d'Alene area. I'm pleased to report his mission is a success. Bob Potter is a great salesman for Northern Idaho and he recruits companies with good benefits programs for their employees in addition to providing a decent wage. As a rule, when Bob successfully recruits a new company, the average annual wage in Kootenai County increases. The benefit of Jobs Plus and Bob Potter is seen in the numbers: 74 companies recruited; 3,780 jobs created; $85 million in new payroll. It is the tireless dedication of people like Mr. Potter that keep our local economies growing and diversifing. Bob Potter's hard work and sense of community should serve as an inspiration to us all, and I thank him for all he has done for Idaho and the nation."*

In addition to the congressional record shown above, on January 9, 2003, Idaho State Senator Larry Craig recognized

Bob Potter by entering a similar account into the 1st session proceedings and debates of the United States Senate.

In response to his efforts to lure manufacturing companies north from the Golden State of California, Potter has been called everything from predator to 'biznapper'. Personally, he prefers to be thought of as a kind of Robin Hood; someone who steals jobs from the rich and gives them to the Inland Northwest.

Bob Potter is a leader in business recruitment and in making a difference in people's lives. His positive impacts on the Inland Northwest will be felt for many years to come and have truly helped shape the future of the region. Still, there may be one thing Bob isn't very good at – being retired. The day after -- yes one day after, he retired from Jobs Plus -- he took a job doing business recruitment for an organization in Eastern Idaho. When he left there, he did some consulting for a couple of months before being hired as the Business Recruitment Director by INEA. Today, he continues to serve in this role at the age of 82 years young.

2. UNDERSTANDING BASIC SALES

Principle: Successful business recruitment starts with system selling – a long term approach to sales.

The master of direct, person-to-person sales, Potter selects clients from manufacturing directories, makes cold calls and then schedules appointments with company owners. He not only sells them on moving their operation to the Inland Northwest but, in most cases, he literally brings the idea to them. And, he does it all the old fashioned way -- with a book, a telephone and an airplane ticket.

Potter describes his method as a *combination of system selling and consultative selling, not commodity selling*. "You need to understand long-term sales and how to position yourself as a consultant for the company," Potter explains. This is why he continues to follow-up with his successful recruits even after they've moved and settled in at their new home in the Inland Northwest.

"I have always sold using this method. I have never known another way to sell," says Potter. "Why was IBM so dominant in the early technology years and today as well? It wasn't the equipment they were selling. It was the approach they were using to sell. They sold for the long haul. As an IBM sales representative, you were constantly thinking about four years from now, not about tomorrow. At AT&T, I tried to get my sales force to emulate the IBM sales philosophy.

"A lot of companies won't take this approach. They won't take the time to train, they won't spend the money they need to spend for training, and ultimately they become too commodity-driven. Companies want results tomorrow, and they aren't willing to wait for results from a long sales cycle," Potter says. "*You have to know more about your customers than they know about themselves.*"

"In recruitment specifically, you need to know the industry you are targeting and the geographic area you are going after inside and out. You need to know the assets and the drawbacks to doing business in that industry and area. If you say the schools are bad or the workers' compensation rates are high, you better know what you're talking about. You NEED to understand what it costs to operate a business in the target area. This is absolutely critical!" says Bob. "Actually, you need to know the strengths and weaknesses of the whole state that you target."

Potter attributes his success to *perseverance and a proven method of approaching small to mid-sized manufacturing companies located in Southern California.* Bob targets businesses that are not location dependent, and he uses a no-nonsense sales approach to encourage them to relocate to the Inland Northwest. Bob subscribes to and thoroughly reads many California business publications, including the regional business journals and newspapers, so he knows what is going on economically and politically in his targeted area. Using hard facts, he shows businesses how they can improve their annual bottom line by leaving California and moving to the Inland Northwest.

He pre-screens companies and sends the prospects detailed information packages via priority mail. Bob contacts the companies, via phone, followed by face-to-face visits and delivery of cost comparisons -- all with the ultimate goal of getting them to relocate – but only if it's truly good for them. Bob finds great satisfaction in working with different companies to solve their problems. "I love selling and proving that what we have here is better than what they have where they are now," states Bob. "To be a good recruiter, *you have to love selling.* For me, there is almost nothing better than to close a case. It is the greatest feeling in the world."

Potter says he has heard the word "no" lots of times. "You learn to live with it; it's going to happen a lot in this kind of selling," Bob explains. "The fun part is the challenge of getting embroiled with the client and getting to spend three or four years with them and then finally watching them open their doors in a new home. Many of my best friends up here are owners of companies I recruited."

Bob Potter mentors other economic development professionals in sales by having representatives from various INEA partner organizations travel with him. According to Paul Anderson, former INEA Board member, "Bob Potter is not just an administrator or an executive director. He is a highly-skilled sales person with a strong financial and business background; he is someone who can connect with people in high places and who feels comfortable making boardroom presentations. Bob loves to pursue and close the sale, and he really works hard to continue to serve the customer after the sale," said Anderson, "He is the epitome of a superb salesperson."

When Bob started selling yellow page ads, he admits he wanted to sell the ads and be done with it. Today, though, Bob is adamant about recognizing the difference between what he describes as commodity selling versus system selling. *"A commodity salesperson doesn't worry about what happens after the sale,"* says Bob. *"With system selling, you get to live with the implementation of your sale forever."*

3. RECOGNIZE THE NEED

Principle: Achieving a high quality of life requires economic diversification to build a stronger and more stable economy for today and tomorrow.

In the early 1980s, the Coeur d'Alene, Idaho, area experienced an economic stagnation that generated intense concern among local businesses and the State of Idaho. Companies in the forest and mining industries suffered massive layoffs, and many of the jobs remaining in the region were minimum wage, service industry positions. Similar conditions were also facing various parts of Eastern Washington, particularly the rural communities.

Remember the old saying "hunger is a great sauce"? Basically, the Coeur d'Alene area was starved. They needed full-time, family-wage job opportunities with benefits. A group of key business owners recognized the dire situation and decided to do something about it. Their answer took shape as an organization called Jobs Plus. "When Jobs Plus was formed, the area was in the tank," remembers Bob. "There was really only one choice, we had to move the economy away from its reliance on natural resource industries, and the answer was to start recruiting. We literally started from scratch."

Grass roots fundraising and strategic planning led to the formation of Jobs Plus in 1987. The business leaders and community members who were behind this major fundraising effort recognized the need for economic diversification and they identified business recruitment as a way to accomplish this goal. Of course, at the time Jobs Plus was formed, an executive director had not yet been identified. It was around this same time that Bob Potter entered the scene.

Potter immediately recognized that the Jobs Plus board was committed to business recruitment and economic improvement for the Coeur d'Alene area in a big way. They had raised enough funds to finance the organization for five years, and they had raised this amount in less than 60 days. What an accomplishment! Long term, Bob knew that the Board of Directors for Jobs Plus needed to be responsible for fundraising. By establishing this requirement up front, two critical objectives were achieved:

- Bob would not have to invest his own time in fundraising which would enable him to focus all his efforts on business recruitment; and
- The continued commitment of local business and the community would be maintained through their own desire to improve and grow the local economy.

Economic diversification is absolutely critical. This was the primary objective of everyone involved from the start of Jobs Plus. Once the board had hired Bob, it was his job to decide how to go about accomplishing this objective. "Not just the Coeur d'Alene area, but the economies throughout the Inland Northwest, need good paying, year round jobs and companies that are good corporate citizens," realized Bob. "All these pieces fit together to strengthen an economy, both locally and regionally."

Bob recalls that he didn't want to diminish the reasons people loved to live in the Inland Northwest, but he also knew that good quality of life can't exist if you're living there without a good job. Perhaps even more important, Bob recognized that jobs alone were not enough. He knew the ultimate goal was to create jobs with career path opportunities that would help keep people in the region and also draw new people to the region.

4. Evaluate Your Assets

Principle: *Know your area's strengths and weaknesses and be proactive about dealing with both in a manner that shows companies you have what it takes to help them be successful.*

How do you evaluate the market you plan to sell? Potter says you need to look at your community or region through the eyes of a corporate site selector. What positive attributes and/or conditions do you have to offer businesses and employees, and what negative elements do you need to address before you go out to sell your community or region?

Potter has faced numerous challenges over the years. When he started as the President of Jobs Plus, the area's schools weren't state certified and negative press about various political scandals were making headlines. According to Potter, these types of situations can be roadblocks to economic development, but only if you try to sweep them under the carpet. Potter recommends being proactive in dealing with major issues that arise. By taking steps to improve or alleviate issues before clients start asking about them, it *shows that your community is proactive and engaged with protecting its reputation and its citizens.*

While temporary press debacles can create diversions and divisions in communities, *the real work is in identifying the true pros and cons of the area, and then addressing the items that are critical to future development.* For instance, in Southern California it is difficult for people to live and work in the same community due to the extremely high cost of living. Take a look at housing costs, the price of gas and commute times. These items alone can make it difficult for a business to find and keep employees.

If you know that these are problems in your target market, *use your knowledge of your own region to develop a market comparison.* In the case of the Inland Northwest, housing costs are still quite affordable. And the region's short commute distances and times can dramatically offset rising fuel costs. In just a quick look at the market comparison on these three items, Potter identifies a clear advantage.

The Inland Northwest is the benefactor of business costs that are significantly lower than those found in Southern California. When Potter first began at Jobs Plus, the combined savings between lower worker's compensation rates and dramatically lower utility rates were almost enough in and of themselves to make the business case. While these two factors still play an important role in proving the business case, quality of life factors such as short commute times and affordable housing are influencing business decisions more than ever.

What about other assets which need to be evaluated? How about your region's education system, transportation assets, manufacturing support systems, workforce quality and quantity, access to capital, and lifestyle attributes to name just a few critical elements? *Business recruitment, the Potter way, is all about providing long-term business solutions, not just for the business itself, but also for the business owners and the employees who work for the business.*

Sometimes it is easier to identify your weaknesses first and then look for strengths. This process is much like the good old-fashioned SWOT (Strengths, Weaknesses, Opportunities, Threats) analysis you learn in business school. Bob sees workforce as the biggest issue facing not just the Inland Northwest, but the nation today. According to national statistics, three out of four high school graduates will not go on after high school and pursue a college degree. So where are they going and how can we get them trained to do technical and trade type jobs? Bob sees this type of training and workforce development as a great opportunity for the area. It will not only help the region's employers, but it will also help the region retain its youth.

Besides workforce concerns, Potter says one of the Inland Northwest region's primary issues to contend with is the outside perception that it can't accommodate, or its reluctance to accommodate, growth of any kind.

On the positive side of the spectrum, the Inland Northwest's attributes are numerous including:

- One-stop small business assistance;
- A flexible community college system, that draws together people utilizing both urban and rural centers;

- Numerous 4-year educational institutions;
- State-of-the-art communications systems;
- A high quality of life – in culture and environment;
- A strong work ethic;
- Reasonable real estate costs and availability;
  (The median house price in Los Angeles County is $560,990; The Inland Northwest is able to counter with a median home price of $170,000 in urban areas and $81,400 in rural communities.)
- Competitive cost of labor (although not too low);
- Relatively low energy costs;
- Abundant and clean water supply;
- Lower lease rates for business; and
- Lower costs for fully serviced land

Potter ranks transportation as one of the most important elements in attracting businesses, especially if targeted companies need easy access to an airport or a major freeway. In the Inland Northwest, Interstate-90, the Spokane International Airport and airports in Coeur d'Alene and Lewiston/Clarkston are great assets to the region. The region also offers rare inland seaports in Lewiston, Clarkston, Whitman County and the Palouse. Plus, the entire Inland Northwest region offers all the amenities of urban living including:

- First class shopping and entertainment
- High-tech medical services
- Cultural events; and
- The nearby perks of a rural lifestyle including incredible outdoor recreation.

"These lifestyle attributes are especially important when you are working with family-owned businesses who might be encountering succession issues between generations of family members," describes Potter. "Family members of succeeding generations have different lifestyle interests and may seek a different quality of life than that of their parents or grandparents. *Bottom line dividends may be only part of what they are interested in. They may also be looking for lifestyle dividends.* This is a lesson worth remembering -- *You must know your client's motivations as well as their needs if the solution you're selling is to be real, meaningful and lasting.*"

What else does Potter see as important assets to use in building a business recruitment program? He says the spirit of cooperation between private enterprise and local governments in the Inland Northwest is the best he has ever seen. This is quite a statement considering how many places Potter has lived and worked. Part of this equation involves the ease of the permitting process. Companies need to know they can get their needs handled quickly and efficiently by the city, county and state entities. "When compared to states like California," relates Bob, "The cities and counties in our region are not difficult to do business with."

One challenge Potter faces in the Inland Northwest is the dynamics of bordering state economies. Interestingly enough, the INEA uses "The Power of Two" as its tagline to sell the region. INEA believes that each state has something to offer and, by offering them both, companies are more likely to move to the area. Certainly, the economy of both states is greatly affected by the economic stability of this bi-state corridor. "But, border economies shouldn't be defined by political boundaries," says Bob. "*The sooner the governments on both sides of the corridor can learn how to improve their cooperation skills, the better off they will both be in the long run.*"

This concept of regionalism is not necessarily a new one; it's just a tough one. In the early 2000's, the Sierra Business Council in Truckee, California reported on a similar approach that recognized cross boundary or border relationships throughout the Sierra Nevada region. In a publication entitled "Investing for Prosperity," the Sierra Business Council had a tactic titled 'Cooperate Within and Across Regions to Address Common Challenges and Opportunities'.[2] This report focused on daily activities that spill across imaginary boundaries and state lines, including trade, recreation and commuting. With new technologies, these boundaries are growing and increasing our range with which to identify issues, generate ideas and solve problems. Old jurisdictional boundaries are becoming less and less important, with everyone beginning to look beyond their borders to work collaboratively to address regional issues and opportunities.

According to Potter, other areas of major importance in analyzing assets include:

- Higher education--The quality of this system is a potential asset that might greatly affect your target industry selection.
- Incentives--Identify what business incentives are available in your area and how they stack up to other

states, especially the ones surrounding your own location?

- Training Programs--Vocational/technical training assets should be evaluated to determine if they are sufficient to meet the needs of your target market.
- People Productivity--A productivity measure needs to be addressed as recruitment prospects are identified. For example, an average commute time of 5-30 minutes depending upon where an employee lives and works is a huge asset and needs to be quantified both for the company and the employee. Other important measures are relative wages and related overhead costs, such as state taxes for insurance and unemployment.

In one of Potter's most successful recruitment efforts, Flexcell (formerly Harper's Office Furniture), he was able to address many of these issues first hand. "Generally, we don't give away free land, but we do have training incentives," says Bob. "With Harper's, *we discovered that we have two state governments and several local governments that can work together to make things happen.* Just like most sports, you got to want it in order to make it happen!" More information on the Flexcell story can be found in Chapter 14. (Flexcell is a business unit of Kimball International based in Indiana.)

5. Identify the Market

Principle: *Outline a recruitment strategy that utilizes your region's assets to meet your economic development goals while providing recruited businesses with a winning business strategy*

One of the keys to successful economic development is having a strategy that makes sense, whether it's based on cluster development or growing the economy one job at a time through entrepreneurship or something else. Once you determine what strategy is best for your community or region, you need to stick to it. This is especially true with business recruitment.

Remember the basic concept of business recruitment is system selling -- it requires a long-term selling strategy and commitment. This doesn't mean you can't have several targets for business recruitment, it really means you should stay focused. You cannot jump from manufacturing one year to high tech the next to medical devices the year after that. However, since you don't want to put all of your eggs in one basket, you may have a strategy that looks something like this:

In order to utilize the region's assets, we will match our workforce skills to target manufacturers who focus on product

> *assembly. Additionally, our region has a growing aging population requiring strong healthcare providers so we will also target medical device manufacturers and medical related software firms.*

By identifying a strategy that utilizes your assets, you accomplish both diversification of your economy and a focus on key areas that are important to your region for long term stability and growth. In today's economic development arena, this strategy might be called cluster based.

Bob targets primarily manufacturing businesses that are not location dependent. He also targets businesses with access to capital and ones that pay their workers above-average wages. "We want to create primary jobs where the company provides a service or makes a product and ships it out," says Bob. "We're not into retail. Retail and service jobs will come later as part of the secondary effect in support of the new jobs brought to the market."

In Potter's experience, the best companies to target for recruitment to the Inland Northwest share several characteristics. They typically:

- Are small to medium sized in terms of number of employees and facility needs;
- Manufacture/distribute a product;
- Market or sell their products nationally or internationally;
- Currently operate in a high cost area;
- Are financially strong;

- Have sufficient capital to finance the move and transition period; and
- Are generally family-owned (simplifying and personalizing the decision-making process)

The whole idea is getting companies that fit the profile. Bob literally hand picks small to medium-sized companies, mostly manufacturers. In addition to satisfying the above criteria, these companies must also meet the INEA employment standards including:

- Paying an average wage that is at least ten percent higher than the current annual average wage for the community being considered as a prospective new home for the company.
- Offer full benefits and career advancement opportunities.

Unlike many economic development organizations, Potter doesn't intentionally target business clusters. "I don't focus intentionally on business clusters, still clusters do happen somewhat naturally as part of the process. I want a company that isn't location dependent, in other words they are footloose," says Bob. "They need to be in a business segment where their costs of doing business will have a significant advantage if they relocate to the Inland Northwest. In the Inland Northwest, the result of these qualifications usually leads to a manufacturing-type business."

If this describes the 'what' to look for, the next thing is 'where' to look for them. In Bob's case, this was a relatively easy decision. "You really need to know the area. You need to know what the assets for the area are, and what the drawbacks are," says Bob. *"You NEED to understand the economic and political situation within the region or state you plan to target. This is absolutely critical!* Plus, you need to know the weaknesses of the whole state. I subscribe to and read lots of publications that focus on California, so I know what is going on throughout the state." Don't forget, Bob lived in California for many years while he worked for AT&T, so it is a little like playing in his own backyard.

In the case of targeting Southern California as your business recruitment market, it is easy to see that the State of California has simply not been friendly to business, particularly when it comes to manufacturers. In fact, a California Department of Commerce survey of manufacturing companies in January 1990 found that 57 percent had seriously considered leaving the state or rethinking business expansions because of environmental regulations. This trend has persisted. In 2001, the California Business Roundtable surveyed California companies and concluded that 14 percent plan to relocate outside California and a whopping 41 percent plan to expand outside the state. "I call on a lot of companies, and often I find that the ones who aren't leaving California are planning to expand their operations outside the state," relates Bob. "Again, I am suggesting to the business owners the idea of moving the company. If they are already planning to expand outside the state, then I have a great head start in my sales pitch."

From Potter's perspective, businesses in California can't do long-range financial or business case planning because of political, regulatory and economic uncertainties. Historically, the legislature just hasn't been dependable enough to rely on for future planning. Businesses that are footloose in terms of suppliers they need and the markets they sell to are definitely interested in a more reliable planning environment. When you combine an unpredictable legislative environment with high worker's compensation costs, high utility costs, onerous regulations, outrageously high housing costs and overall cost of living, its no wonder California has been the prime target for Bob's recruitment efforts.

The six southernmost counties in California represent the largest concentration of manufacturing jobs in the United States according to Jack Kyser, Chief Economist for the Los Angeles County Economic Development Corporation. This makes Southern California a "happy hunting ground" for outsiders looking to entice manufacturers and other businesses to different areas.

"I don't dislike Southern California, in fact I love the area and have spent many years there, but I have a competitive advantage over the area and I am going to use it," explains Bob. Often, he's found that worker's compensation and utility costs are two of the most burdensome costs for California manufacturers and distributors. *Using competitive cost analysis, he shows companies how they can make a lasting difference to their bottom line, recovering the cost of moving in just two or three years.*

PART II

STEPS TO SUCCESS

6. Initial Contact

Principle: *Quickly illustrate the importance and value of the sales call to the business owner, get the dialog started and schedule a face to face meeting.*

The need exists, the assets have been defined and the target market is identified. Now it's time to start contacting companies. Easy -- right? It sounds easy, but let's face it – making cold calls is not on most people's list of favorite things to do. And, how would you like to do it everyday, Monday through Friday like Bob does for the INEA?

Bob starts the sales cycle with potential business recruits by opening the California Book of Manufacturers and the Rich & HiTech California Directories. This is a not a small endeavor as evidenced by taking a look at Bob's book, which is a fully-customized and well-worn version of this publication. Folded pages, notes falling out, clips attached to various sections and highlighted details on thousands of company profiles illustrates that Bob is not new to this practice.

What exactly is he looking for when he opens the book? It all goes back to identifying the target market. Results are critical for Bob and he is keenly aware of the expenses associated with his business recruitment efforts. "I work very hard up front to identify the best prospects," says Bob. "Every packet I send out costs several dollars just in postage, not counting the cost of other materials. I expect to get one appointment out of every ten letters sent, so I can't afford to waste a mailing on a client that doesn't fit the strategy."

So, Bob opens the book and starts going down the page through the profiles. He looks at the products produced, the location, the annual sales, number of employees, the year the business started and the size of the facility. All of these characteristics are important and must fit the target profile. Also among the critical elements Bob reviews are the company ownership and management teams. He looks at the names listed for clues. Does the company appear to be family-owned because the CEO and company have the same name? Are there other management members who have the same last name as the CEO? Based on the year the company was started and the number of family members listed in management, is the business being handed down from generation to generation? These are very important questions for Bob to consider as he picks his potential customers.

Bob doesn't send packets to businesses where he thinks the owners have already made the decision to accept higher costs just so they can live in a nice area. "Quality of life plays an important role in this stuff. If I live in Santa Barbara and own a factory or software company there, it's far different from being down in Anaheim and having an hour and a half commute each way," says Bob.

Bob does not do much if any internet research on his prospects although he admits that at times he wishes he were more proficient on 'surfing the web' so that he could review company websites. "The fact is that I am so familiar with the area (Southern California), I pretty much know whether or not a company is a true prospect or not," says Potter. "The ownership of the companies is important. In fact, some areas have more foreign ownership than others. I avoid companies with foreign ownership. I have found it is difficult to move them into less urban areas."

Potter's first pitch to a prospect arrives in a priority mail package. The package contains a letter highlighting the advantages of doing business in the Inland Northwest and this letter is customized to the prospect's key industry (an example follows). It touts the area's lower worker's compensation rates, substantially less expensive utility costs, lower lease rates and land costs and lower housing costs. According to Bob, it is important to have several different versions of the letter to send out depending upon the industry of the prospect.

But wait, did he say it arrives via priority mail? That's right! *Bob feels that his packages have a better chance of reaching the CEOs or owners of the companies when they arrive in a manner that says the information is important enough to send via an expensive high priority delivery service.* "I think the executive assistant that receives the package is more likely to put it on the owner's desk when it arrives by priority mail," Bob elaborates. "Everyone knows how expensive priority mail is, so it must be important."

In addition to the letter, the package contains a pocket folder with key business, economic and lifestyle information about the region. It's the high level view of the area, hopefully with just enough critical information that the company's top executive will look at it and have some interest in learning more.

Once the packet is sent out, the work really begins. *At this point, Potter must spend a few hours each day making calls. He has to keep looking for prospects to fill the next mailing, while being careful who he sends information to. Then he has to follow up in a timely manner. The cycle repeats itself over and over as the portfolio builds.* Later, in Chapter 10, you'll see how intense the process is once Potter begins making his regular trips to California.

What are the exact steps in the process? *Bob sends out ten packets out at time. Within five days of sending the packages, Bob starts making phone calls.* Once again, Bob denies the obvious benefits of technology. He avoids leaving a voicemail message and he won't leave a call back message with an assistant. No kidding! Bob wants to talk to the owner directly. This is critical to the process because Bob needs that opportunity to begin building the relationship. "I bring the idea of relocating to them. In most cases, the idea of moving hasn't even crossed their mind prior to this point," says Bob. *"Once I get the owner on the phone, at the earliest possible moment, I tell them what I want -- I want you to consider moving your company to my area. I want them to know right away why I am contacting them."* According to Bob this is usually when they audibly gasp in shock over the idea.

As an aside, Bob sometimes gets frustrated with how he describes himself to the prospect. "You only have a limited amount of time to tell them who you are and why you are calling. Right now I lead off with 'Hi, Mr. Jones, my name is Bob Potter and I am the Executive Director for the Inland Northwest Economic Alliance representing … ,' and somewhere in there they realize they have no idea who is talking to them," Bob stresses. "This statement about who I am and the area I represent needs to be something short and sweet, otherwise it's hard to get it out before they hang up on me."

If Bob gets past the introduction, he follows up quickly with the "let me tell you why I sent you our information package and letter" concept. *"I sent this package to you because I felt that you might be interested in what we have to offer, and because your operating costs are so much higher than what we're used to in the Inland Northwest." says Bob. "Usually after the initial pitch, they say, "ok, let's hear what you have to say."*

A one in ten rate of return on this portion of the process doesn't come easy. Sometimes Bob makes ten to 15 phone calls before he finally gets through to the owner. "If I think it's a good lead, I just never give up," says Bob. "I'll call at 6:00 in the morning and try to get them if I have to. Remember, I have already invested the time to identify them as a good prospect and I have spent a good amount of money to send them a packet. I have to make every effort possible to talk to them."

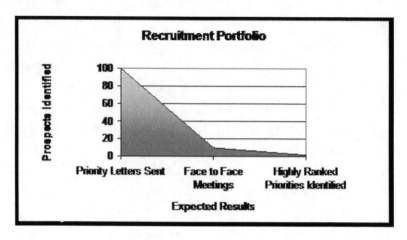

Keeping the dialog alive and open is critical at this point. It is during this initial phone contact that Bob says to the client "I will be in your area visiting in a few weeks, can I stop by and tell you more about the Inland Northwest and why I think you should consider relocating?" *Bob wants the prospect to actually put him on their schedule on the first phone call. He strives to set ten appointments, two per day, all in one week.* And this is how the portfolio begins to develop.

Date

Mr. John Smith, President
My Manufacturing Inc.
1234 Urban Center
Somewhere, CA 00000-0000

Dear Mr. Smith:

My name is Bob Potter and I am the Director of the Inland Northwest Economic Alliance, a non-profit economic development group working to grow the economy and jobs in Eastern Washington and Northern Idaho.

My job is to identify and recruit small to medium sized companies that would benefit from operating in a much lower cost area of the country. I think your company might be a good candidate. Over the last 17 years, I have been responsible for recruiting 70 companies to the Inland Northwest and most are from California. Our latest recruit from California to the Inland Northwest is the Buck Knife Company from El Cajon.

The two largest cities within the region are Spokane, Washington and Coeur d'Alene, Idaho. Within a 100 mile radius of central Spokane, the population base exceeds 800,000. Interstate 90, the main east/west freeway in the northern part of the U.S. runs from Seattle, through Spokane and Coeur d'Alene, all the way to Boston.

Quality of life in the Inland Northwest is hard to beat. We are fortunate in that we live and work in a truly beautiful location. Our neighborhoods are safe; our education affordable; we have leading health care facilities and a welcoming environment for businesses and families.

Our local county and city governmental units are organized to provide efficient and consultative services to both corporate and individual citizens. The region offers a stable and fair tax structure for both businesses and their employees.

In addition:
- Our worker's compensation rates are among the lowest in the nation.
- Our clients can choose between two completely different state tax structures – Idaho and Washington.
- Commercial and industrial lease rates and land costs are a bargain compared to California.
- Our electric utility rates are much lower than you are accustomed to.
- Our region has excellent vendor support for companies that manufacture and need to outsource.
- The Inland Northwest is home to eight colleges and universities and eight community colleges.
- An excellent international airport and an outstanding intermodal rail depot serve our region.

◆ Our region has five port districts with access to the Pacific Ocean.

Above all, there is a sense of community where people that create jobs are valued and appreciated.

I have enclosed a brochure highlighting some of the Inland Northwest region's offerings. If you are interested, I'd be happy to prepare (at no charge) a comparison study that will show you how we can significantly bring your company greater affordability and yield while giving you, your family and employees a better lifestyle.

I will be in Southern California in the very near future and would like to meet with you in person. I'll call you next week to discuss that idea in more detail. In the meantime, feel free to call me at 866-495-8877.

Sincerely,

Bob Potter
Director

Enclosure

A sample manufacturing letter from Bob Potter.

7. The Face to Face Meeting

Principle: *Show the business owner you have a genuine interest in improving their business and get the dialog started – this is the basis for the building of a successful relationship and eventually the move.*

What follows is the author's firsthand account of traveling with Bob on one of his sales missions to Southern California along with excerpts from other economic development professionals who have traveled with Bob.

Traveling with Bob Potter was probably one of the most educational and enjoyable business trips I have ever experienced. I am one of those people who thrive on efficient organization so it thoroughly met my needs. The entire week was planned in detail, maximizing client time while minimizing driving time and filling in unplanned open time with additional client relationship-building opportunities. It was one of the most productive business trips I have ever experienced.

Bob went to work the moment we met at the airport. His first task was to quickly educate me on the schedule and the prospects we would be meeting with during the week. In coordinating trips with Bob, he asks his recruitment colleague (always an economic development professional representing an INEA partner organization) to arrive in California on Sunday evening so they can get started making calls first thing Monday morning. Remember, *the objective is to make ten calls, two per day, Monday through Friday.*

> Bob always does his homework and generally understands the basic manufacturing needs of each company. Always looking for either the support businesses that might be required or the support need that they might be able to supply to companies already in Idaho. You can tell and the owners can tell that Bob is not just making a pitch for their business but really has their best interest in mind. He is always looking for that "Win/Win".
>
> **Michael Sloan**
> ***Director***
> ***Bonner County EDC***

The day before each appointment or in some cases the morning of the appointment, Bob called the prospect to confirm. As he explained to me later, each sales call is very expensive, so he can't afford to have appointments cancelled. Every call is important. Bob even keeps a couple of maybes in mind just in case a prospect cancels at the last minute. I actually watched him make several calls one day during our trip to try and fill a last minute cancellation with a new prospect, and amazingly enough, he did it.

> "Hi Mr. Jones, this is Bob Potter, we have spoken several times on the phone about the Inland Northwest and you have indicated that you might be interested in learning more about the business advantages in our area. As

it turns out, myself and an associate are in your area this week and we have a bit of time this afternoon when we would like to stop by, introduce ourselves, tell you a bit about our area and learn more about your business. Do you have some time this afternoon to fit us in?"

The next thing I know, we have a new appointment scheduled.

> Bob had a strategy for every business we visited. He knows how to take the information they have provided him over the phone and turn it into a "sales pitch" for moving their business here. He works hard at developing a relationship with the owners and staff so they understand he cares about them and wouldn't lead them astray.
>
> **Kathy Parker**
> *Executive Director*
> **SouthEast Washington EDA**

I was nervous as we headed to our first appointment. While I have some sales experience, I don't consider myself an expert by any stretch of the imagination. I wondered how Bob would approach the relocation subject. I wondered how much I would have to participate in the discussion. And I wondered if the prospect would be so shocked they'd just throw us out. The fact is, I worried needlessly. Bob was completely organized and educated, highly professional in his approach and more importantly, *he had prepared the prospects we were visiting so thoroughly on the subject that everything just seemed to fall into place.*

Bob's passion for his work was evident from the moment we stepped thorough the first set of doors. Actually, with Bob, his enthusiasm and passion are always evident. As the prospects came out to greet us, Bob instantly puts them at ease by saying things like "thank you for setting some time aside to talk to us" and "what a great facility this is, how long have you been here?"

Once the formal introductions are made and the usual niceties are out of the way, Bob starts making his pitch. *"Let me tell you why we're here. As I told you on the phone, I want to talk to you about moving your company to the Inland Northwest. We think you might find this move advantageous for your business."* And this is how it all starts.

> **Bob Potter is a wealth of information. Priest River Development Corp. has gained a great deal from his sales mission making the experience enjoyable and well worth our time.**
>
> **Amy McDonald**
> *Priest River Development Corp.*

From here, *Bob asks lots of questions about the company, and he listens, and he listens some more.* He asks questions like:

- How long have you been in business?
- Did you start the company and has it been handed down through the family?
- Is there a new generation positioned to take over?
- How many employees do you have?
- What is your wage range?
- Do you provide benefits?

- How many of your employees own their own homes?
- How big is the facility?
- Do you own or lease it? What about the land it sits on?
- Where do you sell your products?
- What suppliers do you use and are they geographically concentrated in any specific area?
- What support vendors do you require in your manufacturing process?
- What are your monthly utility costs?
- Which classification do you fall under with respect to worker's compensation rates and what is your rate per $100 of payroll?
- What kind of training do you provide for your employees?
- Do you train internally or use an outside source for training?
- Are you able to find employees when you need them and at the rate you are willing to pay?
- And the list goes on and on ...

Eventually, he asks if we can take a tour of the facility. By now, the client is talking away and having fun, and the relationship is already starting to build in Bob's favor. I went on ten calls with Bob and I believe that all ten of them had an interest in staying in touch with Bob, even if they didn't have an interest in moving, purely based on the initial meeting with him. In addition to his warm personality, I saw firsthand that one of the Potter Principles in action. *He actually sells them quickly on something much different than moving – the first thing he sells them on is that he wants to help them improve their business. He reminds us to take a genuine interest in every prospect he meets.*

Once the tour is completed and no show-stoppers have cropped-up, he then asks the multi-million dollar question and it sounds something like this:

> "Now that I've seen and learned more about your company, I think the Inland Northwest area might be a good fit for you. I'd like to start by preparing a cost study for you. If you provide me with just a bit of information on your wages, worker's compensation and utility costs, then I can begin to compare your cost of doing business in Southern California versus the Inland Northwest. Can I start working on this for you?"

This is the key, according to Bob, to keep the dialog going. As long as you have a reason to stay in contact with the prospect, then there is a chance. The relationship will keep building. "I want to walk out the door owing them something, and then when I call them later, I want them to have to get something for me," says Bob. "It is a process of constantly giving each other a reason to keep talking back and forth. *This is the basis of the relationship, because eventually I want them to come to rely on me just as they would rely on their own business consultant.*"

The experience was . . . Invaluable to me, to
learn Bob's strategies and nuances in addressing
prospective clients. Not only were there great
lessons to be learned, but I'm grateful also for
Bob's generous spirit in sharing information and
his genuine thoughtfulness and good nature. It
was a terrific week!

Hilde Shetler
Jobs Plus

A sample client information sheet used by Bob Potter

Bob keeps very detailed notes on every contact he has with each client. While his method may not be as electronically oriented as most people might like to use, his method is extremely thorough. He records, dates, times and content of conversations, mailings or emails.

CLIENT INFORMATION SHEET　　　　Date:　_____

Client Name:　_____

Client Address:　_____

Telephone:　_____　Fax:　_____　Email:　_____

Contact:　_____　Title:　_____

Referred By:　_____　Phone:　_____

Product/Service:　_____

Customer Location:　_____

Current Building Size:　_____　Own/Lease:　_____

If lease, what is rate per square foot per month?

What size building will they need at new location?　_____

Barriers to relocation/expansion?　_____

Number of Employees:　_____　Have they been to area?　_____　When?　_____

Support Vendor Requirements:　_____

Notes:　_____

_____

_____

_____

_____

_____

_____

_____

_____

_____

_____

PRIORITY:　　1 High　_____　2 Medium　_____　3 Low　_____

---

8. FOLLOW-UP IS KEY

Principle: Dialog keeps the door open. The goal here is to increase the prospect's interest in the area and get them to make a visit – thereby continuing to build the relationship.

Potter visits a company at least seven to ten times in person and spends approximately three years bringing the actual move to fruition. In his most recent recruitment success, Bob estimated that he made 15 calls on the company before they even showed any interest in moving. Follow-up is critical in this process so you're top of mind when a decision point arises.

"*The key is to keep the dialog alive,*" says Bob. "*Cost studies keep the client involved.* They keep you engaged by requiring the trading of information. You exchange the cost study and now I have a question and I need to get back to them and then they have to get back to me." According to Bob, "*The most common reason for failure is the result of not getting or keeping the client involved in the back and forth activity.*" However, Bob adds that *another major reason for a company to decline to relocate is the lack of vendors critical to the company's supply chain.* If they can't find suitable alternatives to their established vendor support network, then they simply can't afford to move.

A company working with Bob will get a customized, detailed cost/benefit analysis for its particular corporate structure and a client confidentiality agreement. Bob often uses regulatory issues to build a business case for the Inland Northwest. He compares workers' compensation rates, lease rates, taxes, real estate costs, building permit costs, utility rates--anything he feels is germane to the bottom line for the particular company.

"Once I have them engaged in activity, my objective is to get the company to come to the area for a visit. If I have an appointment, we have a chance to get our foot in the door," relates Bob. "If they make a visit to the area, then we have our whole body in the door. During this entire process, I am always upfront with companies. This is critical. For example, if I tell a company we can give them qualified trainees, we'd better deliver. Otherwise, if we cannot supply the caliber of talent they are looking for, then we are done." *Honesty and integrity is a must in this process!*

As the follow-up process continues, both sides have an opportunity to learn more about each other. According to Bob, this the time when he can make sure the company has the financial wherewithal to proceed. *Bob has turned down companies willing to relocate in the past, because they didn't have the financial strength to make the move.* "I learned that lesson early in my recruitment experience," says Bob. "In fact, two of my failures have been based on this very issue. Usually on my second or third visit to the company, during phase two when I'm preparing the cost study, I will ask them about their financial condition. I have a right to know. I'm putting in a bunch of time, and if a company is in trouble financially, there is no point in moving them."

This stage of the relationship is built upon each side learning more about each other. The business needs to understand what you have to offer that provides them with improved business opportunities. At the same time, you need to determine if your area is truly a good fit for the company long term, and will the relocation benefit both sides of the equation for the long haul? Mutually beneficial results are critical to the long-term success of a business recruitment program.

9. Hosting the Company Visit

Principle: *Understand the goal of the visit and make sure you are continuing to build the relationship by addressing the most important issues facing the client's potential moving decision.*

Once the cost study is completed and the dialog is flowing freely back and forth between the client and Bob, the company may decide to visit the region. A company visit provides the region and communities involved an opportunity to really show off their assets. "If a company decides they want to visit the Inland Northwest," says Bob, "I intend to make sure it is a well orchestrated visit that highlights the best features of the communities under consideration."

According to Bob, sometimes this is tricky. Why? For one thing, the company owner might decide to visit unannounced. This happens quite frequently when you are representing an area that has strong tourist features like many of the communities in the Inland Northwest. The other challenge is time. Often an owner or the company executives will make a visit to the region and have only one or two days scheduled. This becomes extremely challenging when you are representing a large area like the Inland

Northwest. It really forces the host team to focus on only the best and most important features to the client.

Assuming you know the company is making the visit, it is important to spend some time carefully planning how to best showcase your area. At this stage of the relationship, Bob likes to be the main host, but he normally asks one of the partner communities to provide a host as well. *One or two meetings are held to discuss the client, their needs and interests, and critical elements in the recruitment package. Then the schedule is developed. It can take a week or two to get everything organized, so allow enough time to make the arrangements when possible.* The hardest part of planning a company visit is getting all the appointments scheduled with the right people.

A step-by-step look at how a visit is typically orchestrated is presented below.

Checklist for Orchestrating Client Site Visits
1. Prepare a detailed agenda prior to the visit.
2. Upon arrival, meet the client at the airport.
3. If it is early in the day, spend the first couple of hours giving the client a brief tour and overview of the area highlighting features that you know are important to them.
4. Make sure their hotel reservations are at a hotel that speaks to the quality of the area.
5. Treat them to meals at restaurants with great food and excellent service (this can actually speak to the quality of the workforce in the area).

6. Show them the sites of other similar businesses that are in the area, and if possible have them meet with some of these business owners. (This should be prearranged.)

7. Show them land and building options that might meet their needs. If possible, have real estate information organized into a binder for them including sizes, prices, zoning, permitting and contact information.

8. Allow time for meetings with key support agencies/ organizations including city or county elected officials and key staff, the local community college and/or university presidents, staff from employment agencies that might help them with their hiring needs, and economic development professionals from the communities they are considering.

9. If there is time, entertain them with something "local" – a unique golf course, skiing, a local festival – something that gives them a feel for the flair of the area.

10. Visit key support vendors that are critical to their manufacturing process.

The first company visit is your region's chance to keep the dialog moving forward. If the trip is successful, you will likely be hosting several more trips before a final relocation decision is made. "I usually see companies make three or four trips to an area before they make a decision," relates Bob. "Often the first visit will be unplanned and include just the owner and a spouse. The second trip might be the owner and an executive from the company. The third trip might include the management team. And a fourth visit might include key employees that they plan to bring with them as part of the relocation."

Bob tells of one instance where he actually hired a bus and a translator to help with a trip that involved numerous employees of Hispanic descent coming to see the region. The bus toured them through housing developments with realtors. One of the big selling points featured in this recruitment package was that these employees could afford to own their homes in this area, an impossibility in Southern California. It wasn't long after this trip that the company involved announced their decision to relocate and brought these 15 families with them.

Do not underestimate the time it takes to develop the ideal company visit. Bob knows the region forward and backward. He knows who to call, who to put in the room and who to visit. If possible you should do a dry run of your visit prior to the owners' arrival – a rehearsal of sorts. Make sure you know the goal of the visit. Is it to get them to come back again, to select a site, to see the quality workforce, to meet suppliers, vendors, etc? The goal can have a major impact on how you use the time you have available.

In Bob's case, he has already spent so much time building the relationship and getting to know the client that he knows what is important to them. He knows where to take them and what points to get across. He also knows how to entertain them and continue building the relationship for the future. "More often than not, my clients whether they relocate or not become long term friends of mine," explains

Bob. "The clients that have moved to the Hayden Lake area often spend the holidays with Pat and I. We're family."

10. PORTFOLIO MANAGEMENT

Principle: *The goal is to establish a constant flow of businesses moving into the area; portfolio management is a way to achieve this goal.*

Potter has a ten percent return on his mailings from prospects wanting to discuss the possibility of relocating their business to the Inland Northwest. From the very beginning of the process, the idea is to create a pipeline that will continue to build, and result in a flow of new businesses relocating to the area each year.

The portfolio is set up to include all the businesses that are identified as prospects. Once Bob and a member of INEA visit them, prospects are ranked according to the potential for relocation. A company ranked as a one is considered a likely prospect to relocate. A two ranking means the company showed interest in the possibility, but still needs to be sold on the opportunities the move may afford their business. A ranking of three means the prospect is not very interested in the idea and is unlikely to consider relocation at this time. A three ranking does not mean they get dropped from the portfolio though. In Bob's system, he continues to stay in touch and provide them with additional information until they either tell him to stop or he determines that a move would not be beneficial to them.

CLIENT	CITY	ST	BUSINESS TYPE	RANK	VISIT DATE	ACCOMPANIED BY	COST STUDY	CLIENT VISIT	# EMPLOYEES	BLDG SIZE	# OF VISITS	OUTSOURCE OPPOR.
ABC Co.	Anaheim	CA	Mfg	1	01/15/2007	Jane Smith	Yes	Yes	50	12,000	2	Yes
DEF Co.	Los Angeles	CA	Mfg	2	04/20/2006	Jack Roberts	Yes	No	125	50,000	4	No
GHI Co.	Goleta	CA	Med. Devices	3	08/01/2005	Susie White	No	No	15	3,000	2	Yes

A sample of the portfolio form used by Potter.

Bob and his INEA colleague for the week literally discuss the prospect ranking as they leave the business. They discuss their impressions and make a joint decision on the ranking. Once the prospects are ranked, *Bob continues to pursue each one with a single goal in mind – improve the ranking.* In other words, as he continues to follow-up with each prospect, he wants to move each three up to a two and each two up to a one. In the long run, most of Bob's time is spent on getting the ones to make the move decision and getting the twos moved up to ones.

Still, Bob doesn't like to give up on the threes. In fact, he is always looking for ways to help them. Again this is part of his long-term system selling process. As an example, one company Potter visited expressed no interest in moving however they were interested in finding a supplier to assemble part of their product. Bob then set out to help them find a vendor in the Inland Northwest who could provide this service for them. Of course, the ultimate goal of having a one ranking is for the company to make the decision to move to the Inland Northwest.

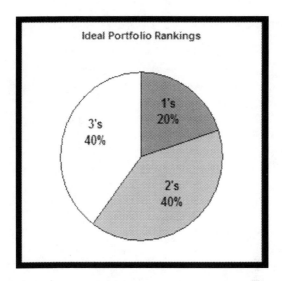

Usually, Bob makes a trip to Southern California once every six weeks. Taking into account holidays or other unforeseen circumstances, this equates to approximately eight trips per year with ten companies per trip for a total of about 80 prospects annually. While the portfolio varies, Bob has a goal to have 20 percent of the prospects ranked as ones, 40 percent ranked as twos and 40 percent ranked as threes.

As Bob works the portfolio through each year, he is constantly changing the rankings according to his continued interaction with each of the prospects. It is a rare occurrence for Bob to actually remove prospects from the list, even if they are a three. Frankly, Bob is a very optimistic person and he is also very confident. He believes that as long as he can continue to stay in touch and build the relationship, eventually he can move the company up in the rankings. In fact, it is not unusual to have Bob make unscheduled stops during his Southern California trips just to swing in and say hi to a prospect ranked as a three. Bob is constantly nurturing the portfolio and he just doesn't give up.

When do you actually take a company out of the portfolio? "If a company tells me straight out, we're not moving, then it's time to get them out of the portfolio," explains Bob. "It's important not to drag them along and waste everyone's time. Still, I find it's hard to let them go after I have invested a lot of time and money in them." Bob admits that he keeps track of all the companies he has dropped from the portfolio and why they were dropped just in case a reason comes up to contact them again.

Portfolio management is essential, especially if you have a prudent board of directors. *"I'm always thinking about what are we going to close next year, and the year after, and maybe the year after that,"* says Bob. *"I want my board to think this way too. They should be asking me what prospects I expect to close during the next one, two and three years."* Bob feels the INEA portfolio is not developing as fast as he would have liked. "I am trying to cover such a large two state area that I am not in control as much as I like to be," he states. "Selling a region is a lot harder than selling one place. That doesn't mean you can't do it. It just means you just have to work harder to do it."

11. THE DECISION TO MOVE: WHAT NOW?

Principle: *A company relocation is a huge project and requires help and support for many years – or a lifetime if you are Bob Potter.*

It's three years, or maybe five years, since Potter sent his first letter to the company. He's met with them somewhere between ten and fifteen times and the company says it is ready to make the move. What happens now?

"When they say they are moving, that is when the real work starts, or at least the second phase of real work," says Potter. "Uprooting a company is very risky and emotional. *The owners and managers will need a lot of help and support as they enter this phase of the project.*"

Depending upon the size of the company being moved, this phase can take anywhere from a few months to a couple of years to complete. "With Harper's, a very large company with 600 employees, we ended up running a year-long training program before the company hired their first person," remembers Bob. "Prospective employees were learning how to manufacture and how to work in a team environment." The move involves many components, some of which are easy to complete and others that are very complicated.

Partial Checklist for Assisting Company Relocation:

- Publicly announcing the move to both the city the company is leaving and the city the company is moving to.
- Finding a suitable location for the company in their new home. This could be an existing building or land where a custom building will be built for them.
- Assistance with the remodeling of a building or the construction of a new building.
- Arranging for the moving of the company's equipment, furniture and inventories as needed.
- Assisting with the purchase and delivery of any new equipment.
- Applying for any machinery and equipment tax credits that are available through the state and local governments.
- Arranging training for the local workforce and/or setting up of local training programs in conjunction with the local education system.
- Working with the client regarding qualified support vendors for outsourcing. (This is especially critical with companies that manufacture aerospace parts or medical device components.)
- Applying for any tax credits or incentives offered by the state for the creation of new jobs in the area.
- Assisting in the process of hiring new employees such as advertising, accepting applications, screening and interviewing of candidates.
- Finding realtors to help with the home search for the owners, managers and employees who are moving with the company.

- Recommending professional services to the people who move such as lawyers, accountants, doctors, dentists, and others who might help them feel more welcome in their new home.
- Making introductions and establishing relationships between the owners and management of the company and key local and state entities that will help insure a long productive business existence.
- Solving any problems that come up before, during and after the move for the company.

A large part of Bob Potter's success is due to the extent to which he makes the whole moving process, as well as the future success, of the business a personal endeavor. Bob literally takes this portion of the project on much as one would take on family responsibilities. In fact, in talking to Bob, he is quick to admit that he feels the company's long-term success is part of his own personal responsibility. "These companies are my family," Bob relates. "Many of them, actually most of them, are our friends and best friends. We spend the holidays together. When they need help, they call me. *For me, the project never ends. I am responsible for them.*"

As an economic development professional, how many people do you think feel this way about the clients they work with? Perhaps this is one of the biggest differences between most selling approaches and the Potter Principles. *Bob makes a lifetime commitment to these companies.*

12. Reporting Results

Principle: Report results that you had a significant impact in bringing about and report them only after they happen – not before!

The results of the business recruitment efforts started by Jobs Plus and Bob Potter are - by any measure -- incredible. In fact, they have been so significant that some people have even criticized Bob Potter's success on behalf of the area because it has grown too much. Bob takes this criticism in stride. "I try to keep in mind at all times that I moved to Hayden Lake for the lifestyle, and I don't want my lifestyle to change," explains Bob. "I don't want to change it for anyone else either, unless of course the change allows them and their children to stay, live and work in the area for a lifetime."

In economic development, it can be difficult to document results of programs. Perhaps that is why so many economic development professionals have coined the phrase 'If it flies over, shoot at it and claim whatever happens to fall to the ground.' Results don't happen overnight, nor are they consistent and often they are not as impressive as the public wants them to be. Plus, results are hard to track at the primary level where they first occur and especially at the secondary level where they are removed from the direct impact.

In the case of Potter, he never reported results to his board or the public until the results were actually benefiting the community. For example, it wasn't until Harper's had hired their first employee and that employee had started receiving wages that Bob reported it as a new job. *Potter feels very strongly that you should only report what has happened, not what is going to happen.* "I never report the jobs, or payroll or taxes a company brings to town until they are actually bringing these things to town," explains Bob. "Generally, once a year I would report to the Jobs Plus board of directors the results for that year. At the same time, I would also lay out the potential for the next one to three years so they would know the status of the portfolio."

Bob doesn't believe economic development professionals should claim successes that they haven't been involved in. "If you say you helped bring a company to the community, you need to have helped them in some very significant way," says Bob. "I think you can get in trouble if you claim results that you didn't really help achieve."

So, what do you actually report? *In Potter's case, he consistently reported things like new jobs, payroll taxes, property taxes and wages.* In reviewing the press Jobs Plus received during Potter's tenure as President, most of these results were published annually.

Interestingly enough, these results only report the primary impact Potter's recruitment efforts had on the economy. Of course, there is significant secondary impact to the community as well. Most economic development studies show that for every manufacturing job created, at least one support job is also created. The real question for an economic developer is how and when to report results, particularly those results that are more elusive. By the way, *Bob only reports the jobs that he directly creates; he never reports the indirect results.*

"Once you get into a recruitment program, you get a lot of synergies happening between different companies," relates Bob. "You begin to try and help them and solve problems for them. *The next thing you know you are helping them with everything from creating succession planning to acquisitions.*"

13. ONGOING IMPROVEMENT

*Principle: Ongoing improvement is about being flexible, re-
evaluating your assets, looking for weaknesses and
changes in the market and the economic conditions
and then updating your strategies accordingly.*

Economic development is never done. You have to continue
to do it everyday; it's not like a water spout you can turn on
and off at will. Economic development, at least successful
economic development, is an on-going process. *The
economic development professional must always be looking for
opportunities to grow, diversify and maintain stability in the
local, regional or state economy.*

Most economic development organization staffs wear so
many hats that sometimes it is hard to remain focused on the
goals. Even more difficult is the struggle that most economic
development organizations have to maintain consistent
budgets without a great amount of effort and fundraising.
Funding for these organizations can range from primarily
public funds to almost entirely private sources. Either
way, it is not uncommon for an economic development
organization to spend a significant amount of time securing
funding on an annual basis. *This is important to note because
unstable funding and/or lack of funding can severely hamper*

recruitment efforts and any level of retention and expansion efforts.

Funding is an area that Bob never took on as a responsibility with Jobs Plus; however, he does participate in this activity through INEA. Why? According to Bob, Jobs Plus was started due to serious economic need and it was started by a group of local businessmen who committed not only their time but their money to the effort. As the Board of Directors for Jobs Plus developed, it was clear from the beginning that while Bob would deliver the results, the Board would take care of securing the ongoing funding for the organization. Fortunately, and one might add uniquely, the Jobs Plus annual budget has been approximately $200,000 since its inception. This small amount of funding covers payroll and expenses for a two-person office and it is a much lower budget than is common for a typical economic development organization.

It is important to remember that Jobs Plus is also focused on only one area of economic development -- recruitment. This focus allowed Bob, as well as his successor, to work toward achieving very specific, albeit difficult, objectives related to bringing companies to the Coeur d'Alene area. Bob claims that this commitment to one type of activity is what truly makes Jobs Plus successful compared to other economic development organizations.

"Look at most EDCs," says Bob. "They wear so many hats, it's impossible for them to find the time, and the money, to be successful at everything. That's why the INEA is so important, especially to rural EDCs. INEA provides an avenue for these organizations that are short of staff, time, and money, to add recruitment to their list of goals and objectives in a meaningful way." *Bob believes that a key component of long-term success for economic development organizations is to properly train other government entities and to rely on other organizations to help pull all the pieces of economic development together.* High turnover in many economic development organizations is a serious problem, especially as it relates to recruiting. INEA helps solve this challenge.

"I look to cities and counties to handle infrastructure," acknowledges Bob. "EDCs need specialists to champion infrastructure development." You need other partners, too. Your local Chambers of Commerce are great for working the retention side of the equation. And hopefully you have an organization, like the Panhandle Council, that can help with packaging incentives, training and grants for you. If you don't, you might need to have the economic development organizations trained to handle these activities. This is critical to a successful recruitment program. *If you don't have all the support in place to conduct these activities, then it doesn't matter how good your recruitment program is. Eventually it will fail because you can't support the businesses that you bring to the area.*

In addition to a great support network, stable funding and local partners, what else can an entity do to help improve their long-term recruitment program? *Ongoing improvement is about being flexible, re-evaluating your assets, looking for weaknesses and changes in the market and the economic conditions.* Then you can revisit your strategy to see if it still fits.

One area that Bob is very concerned with today is the workforce of the region. "When unemployment rates are very low, it can be hard to find people to go to work," explain Bob. "Even when unemployment begins inching up, we still need to focus on our school-to-work programs, our high school technical preparation programs and our manufacturing technology programs, especially those done by our regional community colleges. Here, we have an excellent community college network and we need the whole vocational side of these institutions to be developing programs that meet the needs of businesses in the area." When Bob talks about the future of recruitment, his interest in the availability and qualifications of the workforce receives a significant amount of his attention. Bob emphasizes that it is critical to be in touch with the local job market and knowledgeable of unemployment rates so you can address the workforce needs of your clients.

This is such an important issue for Bob that part of his ongoing improvement for the INEA recruitment package is to find other assets in labor that might be a good fit for his future recruiting efforts. Enter a new target market -- prepackaged software. "This is a very tough nut to crack. It's almost impossible to get to the boss," Bob insists. "But my strategy here is much different than it is for manufacturing. It is not to recruit the company, but instead to convince them to outsource two or three people to work in our business incubators which are typically part of a university. I think this will lower their costs significantly because they can hire software development graduates in the Inland Northwest for substantially lower salaries than those they are hiring in Southern California. And the quality of work they get will be second to none."

Part III

A Case In Point

14. Case Study: Harper's Furniture

It all started in February 1990, when Jobs Plus was using a few volunteers to make cold calls for them. On that day, the President of Harper's happened to answer the phone. "I hadn't even sent out a package yet," recalls Bob. "At that point, he hadn't even ever heard of Coeur d'Alene so it was a cold call in its truest form." Years later, a *Spokesman-Review* article discussing the Harper's move was entitled "Volunteer's Blunder Led to Lucky Find."

Two days after the initial phone call, Bob mailed a letter and packet of information off to the President of Harper's. The letter touted the many virtues of Northern Idaho. The packet was actually a generic cost comparison that Bob received from the Idaho State Department of Commerce. This study compared the cost of doing business in Idaho versus California, Oregon and Washington. It included costs for labor, fringe benefits, worker's compensation and unemployment insurance. This basic report suggested that if Harper's moved to Idaho, they could save nearly one third of these costs.

It wasn't long before Bob Potter made a visit to the Harper's plant in Torrance, California, where he met with the President. According to Bob, the original negotiations with Harper's involved moving only their chair division which had about 50 people. However, as time went by and circumstances evolved, Harper's became serious about moving the entire plant consisting of over 500 workers, and Bob found himself an integral part of one of the largest recruitment projects ever conducted in the State of Idaho.

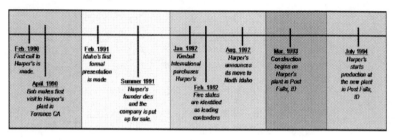

Feb. 1990	Feb. 1991		Jan. 1992	Aug. 1992	Mar. 1993	July 1994
First call to Harper's is made.	Idaho's first formal presentation is made		Kimball International purchases Harper's	Harper's announces its move to North Idaho	Construction begins on Harper's plant in Post Falls, ID	Harper's starts production at the new plant in Post Falls, ID
April 1990 Bob makes first visit to Harper's plant in Torrance CA		Summer 1991 Harper's founder dies and the company is put up for sale.		Feb. 1992 Five states are identified as leading contenders		

"It wasn't too long before the President and I became friends," remembers Bob. "I'd be on a recruiting trip in Los Angeles and I'd meet with him for lunch. We'd talk about things that were going on and how Idaho was stacking up in the competition." Over time, Potter ended up doing dozens of studies comparing business costs among a bigger and bigger group of competitors. While this was a lot of work for Bob, it also had a great benefit for him. Harper's was giving him detailed accounting of their salaries, worker's compensation and utility costs. "This really gave me an inside advantage," says Bob, "Especially as the number of states being considered by Harper's grew to 15 including New Mexico, Arizona, North Carolina, Oregon, Utah and Washington."

As the competition heated up, the President informed Bob that other states were offering Harper's free land and lots of incentives. It was at this point that Bob realized he needed more if Idaho was going to have a chance to successfully land the Harper's business. In February 1991, Bob and a small group of executives made their first formal presentation to Harper's. The presentation went well, but shortly thereafter, Harry Harper, one of the founders of the company, died and Harper's was put up for sale. The president called Bob and said "I don't know where this is going to lead us. So, just put it on hold and we'll see where it takes us." After over a year of working on this project, all Bob could do was to wait.

It was August 1991 when the project resurfaced. Harper's had been purchased by Kimball International and business recruiters across the country were quickly putting together major incentive packages to entice the furniture giant to their areas. Fortunately, Bob Potter already had some big cards showing Idaho's worker's compensation program and an innovative state grant providing a $500 tax credit for every new job created. Potter's package, with these features, kept Idaho in the playing field as it went from 15 states to five in early 1992.

Still, Bob knew it wasn't enough to close the deal. In fact, Harper's President informed Bob that Idaho was currently ranked third and that training funds were the problem. It appeared at this time that the two top states, Oregon and New Mexico, each had nearly $1 million in training funds, and free land on the table. Bob knew he had some serious work to do if he was going to close this deal.

At this point, it is important to recall the relationship building Bob does during his recruitment efforts. Harper's was no exception. His relationship with the President was excellent, and he had already invested nearly two years working with Harper's. In many ways, prior to the purchase by Kimball International, Bob had been serving as their site consultant, doing all their cost comparisons for them. He was operating like an inside consultant on their behalf. This is Potter's preferred mode of operation when it comes to the recruitment process no matter what size the deal. So, what happens next? Well, the Harper's President provides Bob with the proposals from the other states so Bob knows exactly what he needs to do in order to win.

Next on Bob's agenda was to bring the assets of Washington and Idaho together to strengthen his case. First, he approached the two community colleges and asked for their commitment in time and money to deliver pre-employment training to Harper's. They immediately agreed to Potter's proposal. The most difficult portion of this arrangement was how to get Washington to kick in dollars for a relocation that would occur in Idaho. An unusual stipulation was placed on the funding commitment by Washington – half of the 400 plus people that Harper's would hire needed to be residents of the State of Washington. It didn't take long for the leaders in Spokane to recognize the economic benefits that would come across the border from a deal of this magnitude.

While Washington was working through the details of its participation in the proposal, Potter was off working with then Idaho Governor Andrus. Andrus was one of the initial supporters of the Harper's project and immediately committed $150,000 from his own budget. More importantly, he persuaded other departments to commit funding to the proposal as well. In the end, Washington pooled together a total of $435,000 while Idaho gathered

$342,000. Now all Bob needed to stay competitive in the Harper's project was free land.

Bob makes this part sound easy, but its sheer simplicity should tell you it wasn't. After identifying five potential sites, Bob zeroed in on a 30 acre tract of undeveloped farm land in Post Falls. He went to the landowners and asked them hypothetically if they would give him the land in exchange for infrastructure improvements including road, sewer and water hookups to an adjacent parcel they wanted to develop into an industrial park. They said yes. Then he went to the Mayor and City Council of Post Falls and asked, again hypothetically, if they would put in the infrastructure to this property if they could get a manufacturer to build a plant here that would result in a return on investment of about $450,000 per year in property taxes. And they too agreed. "The business case was so good for everyone involved that the only answer was yes," relates Bob.

In April, 1992 Harper's sent two of its top executives to Northern Idaho for a look at the site and the region. Bob orchestrated a detailed company visit including a tour of three potential sites. Shortly thereafter he was able to add a formal proposal from the two community colleges detailing a plan to deliver pre-employment training to Harper's workforce. To clinch the deal, Harper's began receiving letters of support from ranking officials in the cities, counties, states and organizations involved all expressing their commitment to the deal.

The next company visit occurred in early July 1992 just two months after the first visit. But the second visit included three executives from Kimball International in addition to the Harper's executives. During this visit, again the three potential sites were toured, and the Harper's team met with more than 30 representatives from both states, including Governor Andrus, to discuss the pre-employment training package. By mid-July, Bob Potter was asked by Harper's to begin working on the announcement that Harper's was moving its plant to Post Falls, Idaho.

The culmination of the recruitment process, and the start of even more detail work for Bob Potter, occurred on August 25, 1992, when news conferences were held in the morning in Los Angeles and in the afternoon in Post Falls announcing the relocation decision. Prior to this announcement, the entire project had been a closely-guarded secret. Several months later, the President of Harper's said at a local conference that it was the cooperation and innovation of Idaho and Washington coming together that made it work.

Bob Potter was at the center of it all. He brought the project to the table, he nurtured it for years, he assembled key people to get the right cards on the table, and he invested four years in making this relationship happen.

15. Other Potter Lessons

Recognize when you should back off: Potter says that in some instances he realizes that a company shouldn't move; it just isn't right for them. Perhaps the lifestyle attributes are wrong or maybe their commitment to the employees they have is so strong that it would go against their basic business philosophy. "There are definitely cases that I have worked with for a year, or maybe more, and I get to know them and their business well enough to recognize that moving isn't right for them," says Bob reluctantly. "Sometimes you literally have to tell the client that you don't think it is a good move for them and walk away. This happened recently with one of the companies in the INEA portfolio."

Sometimes, manufacturing improvements outweigh or at least equal the actual cost savings: Buck Knives is a good example of a case where this happened. Their cost savings were incredible, and they achieved a major reduction in their manufacturing costs too. After 80 years in San Diego, Buck Knives brought 50 employees and their families with them to Post Falls, Idaho, where they opened a new 128,000 square foot facility. "By combining cost savings resulting from the move and a new manufacturing process, they realized a 30 percent cut in manufacturing costs," describes Bob. "Their worker's compensation bill dropped from $1.4 million annually in California to $150,000 in Idaho." In one newspaper article Chuck Buck said, "It's a new lease on life for our company. A few days ago someone asked me why didn't you guys come up here a long time ago, my only reply was -- I wish we had."

Diversification, eventually you have to do it: Environmental Control was the first significant corporate headquarters Bob recruited to the Coeur d'Alene area. "Recruiting high tech and corporate headquarters requires a different strategy and it's much harder to do," explains Bob. "There are a lot of high tech companies with foreign ownership; there are a lot with very young owners and they have a different approach to business than manufacturing." Despite the difficulties Bob has encountered in trying to get through the door with some high tech companies, he still believes he has a sound business strategy to offer them. His strategy focuses on opening satellite offices where the business can benefit from lower salaries, excellent universities and reasonably-priced facilities.

Working with site consultants, the good and the bad: Potter often finds it difficult to work with site consultants. In general, he describes himself as a bottom feeder, someone who targets smaller companies that site consultants would never take an interest in helping. Remember, Potter is suggesting the idea of moving to the company. Bob likes to be in control of the process, and site consultants like to be in control too. The number of companies that are actually looking to relocate at any time is minute. They have internal teams as well as site consultants working on the relocation project. "I want to be the company's site consultant," says Bob. "I want to be in charge of the process. If the company wants to look at other sites, I will do the comparisons for them."

It can work anywhere: Bob says his strategy and process can work anywhere. In fact, he says he could do it for California in reverse and it would be fun. Bob has already proven his ability to work areas other than Coeur d'Alene and Post Falls. He recruited for Idaho Falls, Pocatello and Eastern Idaho for awhile and of course now he is doing both Eastern Washington and Northern Idaho. "I wouldn't necessarily like doing it everywhere, but I could," says Bob. "Even if you don't have the numbers, you just have to find your assets. Every place has something they can focus on and sell."

Be careful with retail recruitment: Bob worked on recruiting the factory outlet stores to the Post Falls area. "At the time, I felt our tax dollars were going right through town and into Spokane," explains Bob. "I wanted to find a way to get people to shop at home, or stop before they went to Spokane, so we could benefit from those tax dollars." Bob saw his numbers, especially average wages, fall significantly by bringing these minimum wages jobs into town. He quickly learned that retail results are part of the secondary impacts felt by successful recruitment in other targeted industries. Retail doesn't need help. These jobs will come when the time is right.

16. Is Business Recruitment Right for Your Community?

Business recruitment is an extremely competitive field. In order to be successful at it, an organization and a community, county or region needs to understand the role that business recruitment plays in an overall economic development program. When it comes to business recruitment, here are a few key questions a community should address prior to starting a program:

- Why do we want to focus on business recruitment?
- Who do we need to recruit?
- What do we want to accomplish by recruitment?
- Where will we focus our attention?
- When should we start, stop and re-evaluate?
- How much can we spend doing it and for how long?

Economic development isn't all about business recruitment. In fact, recruitment is just part of an overall strategy. This is very important to remember. Twenty years ago, recruitment was thought of as the gem of economic development and everyone was trying to do it. But today, not only have economic development professionals realized the difficulty and expenses surrounding recruitment, but they have also recognized the importance of a long-term effort that involves strategies related to retention and expansion of local businesses in order to be successful.

In many communities, especially the smaller ones where they have fewer assets to market to businesses and less money to spend on recruitment efforts, the key to economic development success has shifted to "grow from within" strategies. This shift for small to mid-sized communities has allowed them to focus more on entrepreneurial and local growth efforts resulting in more diverse and stable economies. One Executive Director of a rural economic development organization with high unemployment and great dependence upon natural resource industries stated, "Growing and diversifying a rural economy one job at a time is a viable strategy and, in some instances, may be the primary strategy to pursue based on financial constraints of the community."

"You cannot forget to do retention," Bob stresses. "Remember, *retention requires a long-term strategy too. You need to position yourself on the very first visit as someone who understands their business and their needs. You also want to make sure they know that you are prepared to stick with them for the long haul.*" Bob identified several companies in need of assistance when he started at Jobs Plus and he immediately went to visit with them. He felt they might move because they weren't healthy financially so he helped them with some of their problems and they became successful and they stayed. "Identifying companies at risk and going to talk to them is absolutely critical for economic development success," says Bob. "This is especially important with family-owned businesses that have no succession strategy in place. Plus, if you are going to start recruiting, *you need to have businesses that are successful in town to provide credibility to your claims about being proactive toward business development efforts. They are built- in references for your long-term recruitment efforts.*"

The "grow from within" strategy in combination with a business recruitment model can be very effective in both rural and urban communities. The model used by the INEA leverages private monies with investor dues from member organizations utilizing a formula based on population. The organization focuses on four main areas including:

1. Business recruitment (led by Bob Potter);
2. Media outreach (executed by public relations firm Hill & Knowlton);
3. Development of customizable regional marketing materials such as brochures, web sites, case studies, photo library, etc.; and
4. Best practices training.

Think about the expertise, knowledge and passion that Bob brings to the table on behalf of the counties that participate in the INEA. A small to mid-sized economic development organization could almost never fund this type of initiative let alone with the Potter-type of horsepower. "The role of INEA is threefold," explains Bob. "*Recruiting, public relations and training, training are what INEA brings to the table. Plus, we bring continuity of personnel and projects to the member organizations.*"

Ultimately, economic development professionals must recognize they have to develop and implement a strategy that includes both internal and external growth initiatives. This is the key to successful economic development. For those areas that are small to mid-sized, teaming up with a regional effort that includes a metropolitan area can be a very efficient way to extend and enhance your economic development efforts, especially as those efforts relate to business recruitment.

Guiding Principles:
<u>Business Attraction</u>

➤ Business attraction is not and should not be the cornerstone of your economic development efforts.

➤ A minimum of 3-5 years is needed to make business attraction successful in a community.

➤ Communities need to know their competitive and comparative advantages before attempting to attract a business.

➤ More than half of business attraction prospects come from within the same state or region.

➤ Manufacturing, while not growing very much, is still a primary target sector for business attraction.

➤ Compiling day-to-day good news of your community and getting it to the prospect can be a very compelling tool.

➤ The most frequently used marketing materials are tailored responses to inquiries, general brochures and fact sheets.

➤ Media advertising, because of its relatively high cost and questionable effectiveness, is the most controversial business prospecting tool.

. . . from A Primer on Economic Development Strategies by
Maury Forman & Jim Mooney

17. Putting It All Together

Is your community ready to implement a business recruitment program? Here is a quick summary of the questions you should ask and the steps used in the Potter Principles:

1. *Long-Term Strategy:* Business recruitment requires a long-term commitment. The selling process involved is system and consultative selling, not commodity selling.
2. *Identify the Need:* Why are you considering business recruitment? Does your community need jobs, diversification, stabilization, recovery?
3. *Know Your Assets:* Identify the positive and negative assets of your own community. Find ways to offset or improve the negatives. What does your community or region have to offer companies? Look for assets that might be unique to your area. What is your community's competitive advantage?
4. *Establish the Target Market:* Utilize your assets, and match the industry to meet your area's specific needs. Don't try to be all things to all people. The whole idea is getting companies that fit the profile of your community or region.
5. *Make Initial Contact:* Once you have a set of companies to approach, make sure you get their attention up

front. Remember, Bob uses the overnight package concept. And don't forget the follow-up! You must follow-up within five days of their receipt of the package.

6. *Set Up Appointments:* Recruitment is expensive, so if you can set-up multiple appointments in a location it will help your budget. It is critical that you are upfront about why you want to meet with them.

7. *Face-to-Face Meeting:* Confirm your appointment the day before and know where you are going so you won't be late. The first thing Bob tells a company is that he thinks their company might be a good fit with his region. From there, listen and learn about the company and their needs and challenges. Tell them about your region and how it might benefit them. The key is to leave the meeting with an action item that requires follow-up to occur. KEEP THE DIALOG GOING!

8. *Follow-Up is Critical:* Once you leave the face-to-face meeting, the work is just beginning. You need to provide the client with some information. And once you do that, you want them to have to provide you with some additional information. This is the stage where the back-and-forth dialog grows and the relationship develops. It is essential that you do what you say you are going to do.

9. *Hosting a Company Visit:* The true dog and pony show! This is your chance to show off your wonderful community. Show the company your best and address any drawbacks with action items to overcome them. Make them want to come back and see more. Plan and schedule this visit thoroughly.

10. *Manage Your Portfolio:* Recruitment is an active, time consuming process. As your portfolio grows, you need to continue evaluating your prospects and your time. If you are spending time with a company that isn't a fit, then take them out of the portfolio. Remember, Bob says his goal with the portfolio is to get the threes moved up to twos and the twos moved to ones and the ones moved to a relocation decision. The goal here is very clear.

11. *Track Your Results:* Because of the time and expense associated with recruitment, you are going to need to be able to show results to your investors. Track the results that are important to your investors. It might be jobs created, wages earned, tax revenue generated, or some other result. Be prepared to remind your investors that recruitment is a lengthy process. It may take you three years to recruit your first company. Keep them informed of your prospects for the future, so they will continue to support your recruitment efforts.

12. *Make Improvements:* As your recruitment program grows and prospers, keep an eye on the economy. Look at your assets and how you compete with other communities and regions. You may continue to focus on the same target market, but you might also need to look at new options. Keep in mind how Bob is dealing with his workforce shortage. Now he is looking at opportunities for satellite offices in software development that can take advantage of the region's strong higher education system. This is a program improvement.

ABOUT THE AUTHOR

A native of the Inland Northwest, Jeni Forman was born in Northern Idaho and raised in Eastern Washington. She received her Bachelor of Arts in Communications and her Master's of Business Administration from the University of Washington in Seattle where she lived for ten years.

Forman has over 20 years of business management experience in both the private and public sectors. After starting her career in advertising where she moved from media planning and buying into account management, she then served in Director of Sales and Marketing, Brand Management and Product Management roles for several large consumer products companies across the country.

Most recently, Forman held the position of Executive Director of a three-county economic development district in rural Eastern Washington. Along with retention, expansion and recruitment efforts, Forman worked diligently on infrastructure development, transportation improvements and enhancement of the entrepreneurial environment in the rural area she represented. She has worked with many governmental agencies at the federal, state, regional and local levels including the Economic Development Administration, the Washington State Department of Community Trade and Economic Development, the United States Department of Agriculture, and the Washington State Department of Transportation.

Serving as the Chairperson for the Inland Northwest Economic Alliance for three years, Forman became very familiar with Mr. Potter and his "classic" recruitment style based on an old-fashioned method of selling. She travelled with him to Southern California where she has seen him in action recruiting businesses to the Inland Northwest.

References

1. Learning to Lead: A Primer on Economic Development Strategies, by Maury Forman and Jim Mooney, Washington State Community, Trade and Economic Development, 1998.
2. Investing for Prosperity: Building Successful Communities and Economies in the Sierra Nevada, A Publication of the Sierra Business Council, 2003.
3. Changing Places: The Story of Harper's Move to Idaho, a Report on the Joint Effort by Idaho and Washington to Recruit Harper's, Presented in the Public Interest by MOMENTUM, 1995.

ACKNOWLEDGEMENTS

The INEA would like to recognize its financial partners for helping to make this publication possible. The commitment of companies like these and others that contribute to their communities' economic well-being are a vital part of helping region's like this throughout the United States.

Founding Investors	Major Investors
Avista Corporation	Bank of America
ICM Asset Management	Qwest Communications
Inland Northwest Health Services	Spokane International Airport
Sacred Heart Medical Center	Verizon Foundation
Sterling Savings Bank	Washington Trust Bank
The Spokesman Review	

In addition, the local economic development organizations that help direct the activities of INEA as well as provide some financial support deserve recognition for their commitment to improving economic conditions not only for their own communities but for the region they are representing. These organizations include:

Northern Idaho:

Boundary County EDC
www.boundaryedc.com

Jobs Plus (Coeur d'Alene Area EDC - Kootenai County)
www.jobsplusonline.com

Latah EDC (Latah County)
www.latahedc.org

Priest River Development Corp. (Bonner County)
www.priestriver.org

Silver Valley EDC (Shoshone County)
www.silvervalleyedc.com

Valley Vision (Nez Perce County)
www.lewis-clarkvalley.com

Eastern Washington:

Greater Spokane Incorporated (Spokane)
www.greaterspokane.org

Lincoln County EDC (Lincoln County)
www.lincolnedc.org

Port of Whitman County (Whitman County)
www.portwhitman.com

SouthEast Washington EDA (Asotin, Columbia, Garfield, Whitman counties)
www.seweda.org

Valley Vision (Asotin County)
www.lewis-clarkvalley.com

A special thanks also to Bob Potter and Sharon Matthews, INEA Executive Director, who spent countless hours answering questions, responding to emails and reviewing the facts presented here. Their efforts brought the *Potter Principles* together as a source of best practices for business recruitment across the country as well as for the true sales enthusiast who is committed to long-term sales success and customer satisfaction.

For more information on INEA visit their website at www.inlandnorthwestregion.com.